# Previous Praise for Peter Weltner's Writing

"Read it for the power and sanity of a poet in his ripeness: there is much richness here."

*Maxine Chernoff*

"Weltner's agile, passionate ear guides and clarifies imagination, as the poems' emotional truths dance to an intricate, organic music, delicate, tidal."

*William O'Daly*

"These poems look directly at the world. They don't flinch in the face of loss and death. They strive for a transcendence where 'All's light. All's water. All's paradise shimmering.'"

*Joseph Stroud*

"These poems enact a powerful unbecoming of time, momentarily halting its flow so that the silent preciousness of the past becomes audible."

*Jason Wirth*

"Finds love and passion in the sea, hunger in dust....I feel breathless and sad that the world I live in doesn't care or is avoiding the size, scale, bounty, moral rigor, and passion of our lives that can be found here."

*Linda Gregg*

"Weltner confronts the reality of a zone poised beyond the limit of death conveniently drawn by us."

*Kathleen Fraser*

# LATE THOUGHTS

# LATE THOUGHTS

Poems
PETER WELTNER

MARROWSTONE PRESS   SEATTLE

*Late Thoughts, poems* by Peter Weltner, © 2019
All rights reserved,
Marrowstone Press, © 2019


ISBN: 978-0-578-61272-0


cover image: 'Elegy for Linda,' oil on panel, by Galen Garwood, 2019

To Manhattan and All Its Artists and the Visions They Gave Me
Growing Up in the 'Fifties

Table of Contents

## I.

The Sixth Day of Creation   *1*
Sometimes There's God So Quickly   *2*
Ocean Drive   *3*
Ursa Major   *4*
Forty Years   *5*
Prayer   *6*
The Flood   *7*
Vigil   *8*
Fire Sermon   *9*
Denmark   *10*
Prelude   *11*
At Ten O'Clock in the Morning   *12*
Home   *13*
Thirteen   *14*
In Place of a Benediction   *15*

## II.

Santorini   *19*
Agamemnon   *20*
Naxos   *21*
Lemnos   *22*
Mycenae   *23*
The Return   *24*
Memnon   *25*
Rome under Siege   *26*
Centurions   *27*
Roman Fever   *28*
Exilium   *29*
Love in the Days of the Caesars   *30*
Sulla   *31*
Istoría   *32*
Antiquities   *33*

## III.

Evil as a Force of History  *37*
One Day in History  *38*
Walter Benjamin  *39*
On Tragedy  *40*
Home Front  *41*
Numbers Sanctify, My Good Fellow!  *42*
A Border Trilogy  *43*
Migrant  *45*
A Mother and Her Son  *46*
Tikal  *47*
A Reliquary for Juan Carlos  *48*
Alejandro Saves Himself from Drowning  *49*
Lawrence's Plumed Serpent  *50*

## IV.

Canticum Sacrum  *53*
Murillo's After the Flagellation of Christ  *54*
Lear's Fool  *55*
Fryderyk  *56*
February 13, 1883  *57*
J. M. W. Turner  *58*
Kafka  *59*
À Jarry  *60*
Ferrara's Pasolini  *61*
The Movie Version  *62*
Out of the Past  *63*
Linda's Kore  *64*
Parade  *66*
Curricula  *68*

## V.

Ground Fog  *73*
Childhood Scenes  *74*
A Boy's Secret Garden  *78*
First Communion  *79*
Altar Boys  *81*
Listening to Ives with Bob at Ojai  *82*
Rice Wine  *84*
My Husband's Garden  *86*
Free Variations on Two Parables by Antonio Machado  *87*
Notes I Never Wrote to My Father  *88*

## VI.

After Sappho  *93*
A Medieval Manuscript of Job 2:9  *96*
Noche Oscura  *97*
Schumann, Fantasie, Op. 17  *98*
Acrophobia  *99*
Another Twilight  *100*
Learning Reverence  *101*
The Day  *102*
Young Oedipus in Corinth  *105*
A Last Heron on Hamilton Lake in Late November  *106*

I

# The Sixth Day of Creation

*1.*

Today, nothing less than paradise suffices. Waves breaking over rocks,
tugging shell shards, pebbles into slim tidal sluices,
washing the sand where loggerhead turtles lay
their eggs. Gulls, pelican flocks,
sandpipers made radiant by how the sun as it rises
sanctifies all things. Laurel oak and live oak, sweet smelling bay,
hornbeam, ironwood, flowering dogwood, red cedar.
In the wetland swales glow-
ing red maple, cattails, marsh grasses.
Red-tailed deer, wild goats, musk deer delight in shade and shadow.
In spring the warblers come to mate from far
away. Hawks and other raptors follow,
belong here, too, in pursuit of food while you and I, like one,
walk hand in hand along the strand on the sixth day of creation.

*2.*

Thirty years after, I can still smell,
feel, taste him on my fingers. Sweat. Seed.
Specks of blood maybe. I couldn't always tell
before what was his, what mine, freed
by passion from the need to decide. Some of his clothes
live on, hanging in my closet. The music
he favored plays in my head. Who knows
anymore how kind he was then? How good? How beautiful until he fell sick?

The Greeks were right to be frightened by their gods, Eros
most of all. Tragedy is not melodrama, an ecstasy
of apprehension. It is the loss that follows you, goes
wherever you go. It is the ordinary
holy things he has left behind, a stack of books, baseball cap, black
leather jacket, college ring, faded white briefs that beseech me, calling me back.

**Sometimes There's God So Quickly**

A small beach, its gritty sand brittle as dry grass. A lake,
rippling through reeds, slapping against the cement pier
beneath a diving board. A solitary garter snake.
Jasmine. Magnolia. Roses. Their perfumes belong here
with me now. House lights flickering off the calm water
mallards drift on drowsily. White sheets of clouds
veiling a waxing moon. A dam, its overflow stir-
ring the slow creek below it. What the past enshrouds
memory revives. A car door slammed. The humid air
dew-heavy. His naked body like mirrored light, the glow
off gold, the patina on bronze. An August late night is smiling
down upon us with its usual ironies. What two boys dare
by desiring. Eyes that meet in secret and know. So
it is not paradise. Yet call it grace. Call it lives suddenly beginning.

**Ocean Drive**

A manic summer storm out of the east breaks through the middle of the night,
wind gusts rattling windows, thumping, shaking doors, high waves
shattering stairs and slats of the pier. It is all right,
John. Dream on of lost wildernesses, of jewels hidden in caves
as you told me you do nearly every night, no peace
from your repeatedly dreaming your one way to escape. I don't regret
my crush on you, despite your "No" or your sleeping through the tempest,
brief as it proved to be. I don't lament what I confessed to you, though sunset
feels like many days ago. You just need some sort of sexual release,
that's all, you said, after I tried to persuade you the best
of me was my love for you. You counted stars in the constellation of the Great Bear
out loud, recited to me a few of their names. Went to bed. The earth's silence,
its clarity after a cleansing storm should make humanity ashamed. The stars glare
down on me brighter now it is near dawn. And on you, lying oblivious by me, in all your
    magnificence.

## Ursa Major

Another brief storm, a reminder in the middle of a late life night,
wind gusts again breaking like waves
against windows and doors near an ocean.  Is it right
for me to be dreaming of wilderness, of precious things hidden in caves,
of childhood-like escapes as you once did?  Isn't forgetfulness peace,
like a storm retreating to where it came from?  I no longer regret,
do I?, the time you told me, "No."  Don't rains release
the heavens by falling?  Doesn't every good day darken at sunset?

Backpacking in woods when I was still young enough, a downpour over,
in your honor, I tried to name the wandering
stars in the constellation of the Great Bear.  The courage
of a moment is like an eclipse of the moon, something
difficult to describe after
it is finished, a passion I turned my back on, an infatuation collapsing like a happy
    marriage.

**Forty Years**

Twilight smolders like wild fires dying on a mountain peak.
Shadows fade from my bedroom while night floods in.
Shining through a window, the moon would shame me. I speak
to it candidly, admit to it that when
my friend died, yes, I refused to listen
to its consolations. How much longer
must I bear it, I had asked it, growing older
than he ever would? And he only one among so many men.

A year after he got sick, he told me (yes, on the shore of a lake
left starless by a sky
shrouded in clouds), my dear friend, the kind man
now dead for forty years, for whose sake
I must never forget anyone, he said, who never would lie
to me, someday I'd be at peace with it, someday I'd understand.

**Prayer**

Lovely, kind
man, you who fed the hungry,
healed the sick, would have given sight to the blind
if you could, comforted the mortally
ill, consoled those in despair,
you, who abandoned your family
for the sake of others, be merci-
ful, rectify
my errors, who showed while dying that fear
of death is also holy,
my dear
friend, help me be free
of terror, who would say, "Come see,"
as you displayed for me like a sign to read the newest sarcomas bruising your body.

The Flood

Silt-smeared photographs. Shattered vases. Soggy faded family papers.
Cracked glassware. Smashed cabinets. Shards of earthenware plates.
Revive the Heraclitean question. Which way is up, which down? The river's
become a sea. Houses rent. Shutters scattered. Twisted gates.
Trees entangled with carcasses. Stumps like mud-men in a swamp land.

Blue ribbons on a beheaded doll. Stacks of flattened hats. The unplanned
for future, the deluge's residue of the once good and happily visible.
Snapped train tracks. Drowned factories, car parks. Washed-out crops.
Inundated cities. Impassable roads and lands. And I, like Ishmael
saved from the sea, come back, storm-shocked, the moment it stops,

dazed, wandering after it is over, crossing into
an unknown country
of some permanent ruin, I, unlike Noah refused
the Lord's magnanimity
(if that is what it was), like Ham disabused
of Jahweh's promise to the redeemed, still seeking the rainbow banishment is due.

**Vigil**

The moon is a fat, burnt orange, a harvest moon
in the middle of April. Two nights ago, the seder.
Friday, the crucifixion.
Rain then with more rain to fall later today, strange weather
for spring here. A cold
wind from a cloud bank blows
from off shore. Frightened thrushes scold, bold-
ly attack a cat prowling through shrubs. A truck with a broken muffler
belching smoke rattles down the highway. Two homeless men doze
snoring on a cement bench. Afraid of water,
a dog barks at high tide. A fire burns on the beach, the stink of rot
and old tires in its smoke. Why am I not sleepier,
more exhausted? Why I am watchful so long when I am not
a believer? And yet I wait. I anticipate. Beset with grief, vigilance, my lax redeemer.

## Fire Sermon

A black-spotted tokay lizard killed
by a cat it was made to fight,
smothered by ants, feelers alert,
hungry for gecko, appetite-willed
by a need to survive, as night
must ever devour day, not hurt-
ing it further, the lizard's life done
for already, finished, each insect red as flames
smoldering, burning like Buddha's Fire Sermon:
not desire disappear-
ing like smoke from a pyre by the holy river,
but the fear
it kindled as your lover
afterward chants in your ears your secret thousand sacred names.

## Denmark

Before dawn, beachside
by the Baltic, in a dream,
I strip, swim toward a small island wide
from shore in water cold as a mountain stream,
crystalline blue
like ice floes in midwinter.
I claim the island is you,
Carl, lying further
from shore than I dare swim to. Yet I do though the surf
grows rougher, overcoming what strength
I have left. I try to tread water. For all I am worth,
I fight against the currents, the surging tide
that drags me under until I died
in the dream, in the ecstasy we knew, the sea's unfathomable depth.

## Prelude

Since nothing living, wild, tame, enchained, free,
fed, hungry, safely settled in country, in towns or cities,
wandering over land, roaming by air or sea,
since no one, nothing is spared mortality's
fate, whatever histories write, what monuments
display no more than passing reminders
of what once was, signs of what the spirit invents
and for a while remembers
like conjurers of spells, like magicians
evoking another fantastic story–
and yet, though all this is so, since today the sea's breezes are as saltily
sweet as the incense of smoldering rose wood and glory
is a sky opening to the sun as a meadow of black-eyed susans
and Wood's blue asters unfurls to first light, I say, with Wordsworth, Take me,
   change me.

## At Ten O'Clock in the Morning

Scattered clouds. Scimitar-sharp,
a new moon slips into the sea.
A frail man strolls along the beach
in no hurry, keeps watch for a while.

A boat beset by gusts is warp-
ing against the wind, no longer free,
tied to sea-anchor, breach-
ing the calm until tugged safe to sail.

The old man stands by a rail on the shore,
listening for the call of a boy
he once loved, drawn to the past,

leans on a pole for support. What more
might he gather from the joy
of lost days? Paradise. Each instant unsurpassed.

**Home**

The splendor of trees in a springtime greening, leaves
pale jade, deep chrysophrase,
the cloudy sky a gray crystal bowl.  Church bells sound
as if from far away in praise
of Sundays of peace.  Wild flowers
bud and blossom in an overrun garden.
Pink and white dogwood showers
petals onto ground
sodden from mist and rain,
the breezes resinous as pine woods.  How do you sustain
the lost places of youth, its half forgotten
meadows and creeks, its forests visible as photographs
or a Japanese screen on which a gray bearded sage, gape-mouthed, laughs,
his pastoral dream of returning home fleeting as the stream he poles his skiff on?

**Thirteen**

In a spiral pad, a boy sketches his father
who breaks into a smile while fill-
ing a basket with Adam's roses to offer
his wife. There is an autumn chill
to the looming clouds. He draws and draws,
yet can't portray,
can't accurately trace the faces of others. A cat claws
at the screen door. Or is it just play-
ing with a bug? Honeysuckle clings to the gate.
Hollyhock blooms late by the swings in the backyard.
The boy is trying to contemplate
his future, what fate might make of him later. The air is hazy
and sweet. A handsome carpenter is hard
at work, hammering nails into a new deck. Puberty. What truths it makes him see.

## In Place of a Benediction

A crumbling, dangerous shelf lies beneath the Atlantic,
a reef many ships have wrecked
on that shifts tides,
affecting currents. He resides
yards away, fills his days roaming the coast in search of shells
and driftwood, an old cranky scavenger. Swells
recently have reached his backdoor threat-
ening what he would claim is the last seedy house inhabited still in Amagansett.

Last night, he phoned to tell me he had found a red rose
with a long stem in a crystal vase addressed
to him that someone had placed on his porch, who knows
why. He felt, he didn't know how else to say it, blessed,
he supposed, by a gift he'll never forget
after living impoverished for so many years in the last shack standing in Amagansett.

II

Santorini

The island is a graveyard of scattered shard chips,
bone scraps and slivers, old coins, ancient graffiti.
In the valley, oblivious of the past, a new born lamb slips
on mist-slick weeds.  Greedy
for life, it suckles on its mother's teat
as a cruise ship sails out of the harbor on
its way to another port.  Morning heat
seeps into rooms and clings like dew.  A fisherman shivers in the sun.

The women who live here whitewash their houses, sweep
cobblestone walkways with brooms made
from brush and twigs, gossip.  The men fish, repair
ropes, play cards.  History is everywhere,
yet silent.  The island is curved like the battered blade
of an unsheathed scimitar.  For four thousand more years let it sleep, let it sleep.

## Agamemnon

Murmurs of Troy-bound winds, the calm sea a mirror of an ephemeral peace, another black freighter
on its way into harbor. The mountain near
the olive groves is bald as a church dome. Older
than the gods, wrapped in shawls darker than night, women
cross themselves in its shadows. At sunset,
it gleams and blesses no one. A small airplane
flies in new tourists. To find a few gold coins. A spangling trinket.
Pursue rumors of gold. I climb to the wind-sharpened rock
on the summit of a lesser mountain,
cup my hands in a pool of rainwater
to perform my morning ablution. On the dock
far below, fishermen empty their catch from their nets. Again
the net. You and I trapped by the same wide net, my daughter.

**Naxos**

A boy watches the sea off Naxos, even young-
er than the god he prays to,
hums to his deity a song sung
to him by the moon. You
weep before
such beauty with a stranger's tears,
abhor
your wasted years. It's a hot afternoon. You cruise the piers.
A horned grebe flies over an olive tree's
branches. A fisherman's boat
sails the sea leaping waves lithe as a dolphin. The flayed skin of a goat
dries like old clothes in the heat of a breeze.
It is Greece, ancient Greece, the wonder
of first things, that maddens you. The god you pursued one golden sundering summer.

**Lemnos**

Yesterday, in an open field by a desolate olive
grove, I found a marble shard I pocketed
for luck. Who does not long to live
forever, like a poem read
down through the centuries? I eat melons,
figs, and dates. Little more.
I know when I die you will pour
wine on my grave, offer lemon cakes and honeyed almonds.

I fantasized last night my body had been left on an island,
my suppurating foot stinking like scat,
though wrapped in a bandage.

The ancient Greeks believed that every language
begins in mourning, ululations. A tragic bat-
tle awaits my bow. Grieve for the living none dead understand.

Mycenae

Rocks and vines drip drip like a broken faucet.
At the precipice of a sheer cliff, a stream
flows into a waterfall. It is near sunset.
Wind-shaken leaves sparkle like earrings, gleam

brighter as light fades. The cascade surges, crashes
onto the beach. Near my age, a man stands
at the edge of a grove, picking olives, stashes
more into his bulging pockets. Green bands

of leaves form a wreath, a crescent round his head
like a crown of laurel and bay. Stone walls.
Iron gates. Gold masks. Carved lions. Instead
of him, it is myth I am entering. Ancient halls,

their bronze doors. He shivers in a seaborne chill,
his face like a marble statue's near a fountain
at the foot of a mountain that wine would fill
as abundantly as streams teem after rain.

Hazy brush. Outcrop filmy with mist. Vines.
A dusk woven with gold strands. A palace threaded
with twilight. Who offers the rites, who dines
with us at our feast? Apollo, beauteous and dreaded.

## The Return

It is shortly past sunrise, but no birds are singing,
not yet. It is cold for Greece, the fog, pale white,
slowly receding to the sea, a bitter chill stinging
his eyes as he stares out far past the rising half light.

Off shore winds sound their own mournful music.
He looks down at his young man's hands,
surprised, no doubt a moment's trick
of the mind, after a man has died, no one understands.

How much the wilds of Paros appear to be the same
as the stormy day he left it decades
before, only hard weather left to tame
mountains, no more wanton gods, pirates, crusades.

So this is where the end has brought him, to the island
where, it is possible, his poetry began,
to the ancient women, black hair sandgritty,
exposed skin, clothes filthy, crag-faced fisherman

husband bound to the sea's cruelty, harsh life,
men they know one day they will weep
and weep for, a widow, never more a wife,
silently sweeping the tiered white steps, the steep

paths before the white-washed houses while waiting
for them to return, tragedy's
origins, or one of them, in the common pain
of the daily, primordial, the meaning the poet sees

is his own, is everyone's, an old woman dressed
head to toe in night black, staring out, out
beyond sight, far past the horizon, blessed,
he supposes, alive still, still hoping, ever faithful, ever devout.

**Memnon**

At dawn, the Colossi of Memnon sing a harmonious
plaint, as at the end
of a tragedy.

Pilgrims gather in the intense desert heat to hear
its entrancing music, to learn
of what it prophesies.

Sometimes, Eos, luminous goddess, strikes the massive
stone statues of Amenhotep
in lamentation,

a grieving mother, keening each morning
for the son she lost, slaughtered
by Achilles at Troy.

Blocks of quartzite sandstone, quarried at
el-Gabal el Ahmar, sound
her sorrow,

the paradox of daybreak when dreams of paradise
are awakened by the stronger songs
of the sun.

**Rome under Siege**

Devotees of Cybebe, you come
unbidden, unwelcome to Rome,
the city you'd destroy-
with timbrels, flutes, drums, crotales, cymbals.
Slashing flesh. Imbibing wine.  Nothing
forbidden, the mad joy
of mobs desecrating order.  Plaything
of the goddess, you prey on each other like beasts.  Cabals
and plots race fast as assassins from circus to forum.

City of decrepit old age,
of ghosts and visitations,
fears, premonitions,
lies and misprisions,
abiding every violence,
dying of resentments and rage,
tell me, how safe do you feel hidden behind the walls of your own Olympian silence.

**Centurions**

Medes overcome. Barbarians.
Gelonian bowmen
pacified. Ten
years of fighting. Two centurions,

more like lovers. Battling Goths in wolf-toothed
forests. Armenians
across deserts who, massive as loosened
boulders, fell on them from snow-peaked mountains.

Lion-maned Parthians
effeminately
armored in baggy trousers. Set-faced Egyptians.
Dolphin-sleek sea-

people. Boar-bold warriors
in oak-dark Germania.
Stone-hard, naked berserkers
in moon-maddened Britannia.

So many fellows killed. Gaius, Rufus,
Marcus, Felix,
Demetrius: skin yellow as pus,
lips blue as bruises, white eyes, death-shriveled pricks.

And Palestine, the terrors
of the crucified,
eyeing their executioners,
traitors who died spied

by hawks, vultures
ravenous for carrion,
the stink that lures
them, beaks clacking, hungry for bone.

The shock of history is theirs
as if each were a Carthage
under siege, no prayers
to the gods undoing our war's carnage.

## Roman Fever

Along the craggy shoreline
where your days ended,
Marcus, I pour the sacred wine,
the libation you said
was mine to choose that you might rise
out of waves, the cries
of island birds, the sea that buoyed you
starward. I honor the rite, your plea never
to be forgotten, Brother. So
I vowed two
thousand years and more ago,
citizen of Rome, eternal city,
while waves rocked you sleeplessly
to sleep in my arms, crazed by fever, wanting water.

**Exilium**

On a deserted shore of empire,
foreboding and Mediterranean,
its searing heat, I tire
of temple, altar, one by one
beasts being slaughtered,
the feast to follow, on slaves' shoulders
roast boar brought to table, dried
men like me garlanded with grape leaves, stinking of scented waters.

Banished when young, we find our hair
has grown white as our togas once were. We savor
what wine we are given. Nonsense
is the stuff of poets dar-
ing to criticize Caesar, bor-
ing each other, allowed to survive for our art's inconsequence.

## Love in the Days of the Caesars

Why did you turn your back
to me when last
we met in Ostia, Rufus? You know
Flavia lied. Why did you feign
sleeping so late? Why did I pay
a drachma to an augur
to say, "Sacrifice
to Bacchus," after
we already had screwed
late into the night,
licking sweat like the wine we had spilled on our bodies?

Our cohort must ready itself
to leave Rome, to fight once more
on the Parthian or Dacian border,
to depart from the city
that is the myth of us, of our love.
I write to you what Catullus
refused to say to Juventius:
that you and I, Rufus, must be traitors
to power, to emperors,
to the imperial order
we make war for and flee from.

Let us from Brundisium sail not to Capri
with its Tiberian orgies
but to Samos, Thessaly,
or the shores of the Caspian Sea
where the sun rises each day
like you out of bed
to reveal the Elysian peace
we declare between us,
the new Rome we'll rebuild
as if from Parian marble
on the Palatine Hill of our rapture.

# Sulla

Gaius is dead, Lucius, noble companion, yours and mine, of our wars against Mithridates who slaughtered eighty thousand Italians, the Asiatic tyrant our dictator has let go, returned to power, promoted. Deceitful Sulla who after our victories marched on Rome to prevent the Italians from receiving the equality they had been promised.

What should we have expected of a man who had sacked all of Athens, looted Delphi's treasury, who'd bragged he had come to Attica not to learn its history but butcher its people? Believer in omens, oracles, visions, yet defiant of the gods. Killer of Roman citizens who'd resisted his power on the Esquiline Hill.

He who displayed Sulpicius' head on the Rostra. Who had an elderly neighbor and friend who had broken with him tossed from the Tarpeian Rock. Who at the Circus of Rome massacred a thousand Samnites whose dying cries echoed through the Temple of Bellona while he smugly lectured terrified senators on his great victories in Pontus.

How many did he slay? Sixty? A hundred bloodied white togas? Sixteen hundred equites? When did it begin, the fall of our Republic? Long ago, I suppose, the day two generations before us Tiberius Gracchus was clubbed to death in the streets of our city.

"Quit quoting laws to us," says Pompey, "who have swords to wield." Restless legions have replaced the Republic, Lucius. Our Gaius is dead, my friend. And like him for whom he was named, Gaius Gracchus, I mean, Tiberius' brother, he dies again and again.

What have we lost? Mos maiorum, the way of the elders. Customs, unwritten rules, communal hopes and dreams, bonds we Romans let be placed upon us, accepted for the good of the state we'd inherited.

No more civitas, suffragium. No more consuls, tribunes. Only Sulla, executor of the laws he has dictated, he claims, not for himself, not to enrich anyone, but to restore the ancient Republic, the old city, the old sacred Rome, the old laws he has revived by maintaining through his lies a new brute order of violence.

**Istoría**

My island lies close to the Trojan coast. At night, I try
to revive its invaders in my mind. Turks, Crusaders,
Templars, anchorite monks, Venetians. I
am weary in spirit. At the limit of reason, at water's
edge, I confess
I know nothing. Small boats tied dockside
rock like cradles. Forgive me my gracelessness.
The women here wear black all year to let men know how they have survived.

I enjoy listening to local stories, Greeks
the first historians, but remember
them only in fragments. A summer storm
climbs over mountain peaks,
obscured by clouds. I am a teller
of tales, of ancient tragedies' bits and pieces. How all men come to harm.

Antiquities

Death is indifferent in its immensity.
It stupefies
the mind with its cruelty,
defies
language. Take a daily
walk along a beach. A crow pecks at the carcass
of a gull, bloodies
the sand. Fish heads, crab shells, a dead rat lying in dune grass.

Tell me again the story you told us all last night.
How, on a mountain in Lesvos,
you found a shard of a kouros
you fell in love with at first sight.
How you kissed his lips, sun-warm and inviting.
How your blood quickened. Why you feared nothing.

III

## Evil as a Force in History

Her village is almost invisible now,
its inhabitants long gone,
its earth sterile.
Never to be done
with labor, she works in her garden,
picks a shriveled
tomato from an infested vine, eats. When
it is night, she keeps the shades down, bedeviled
by fear. Like snakes,
she craves a hole to hide in, her bones
brittle, easy to break. History takes
on a bitter face if no one atones
for its catastrophes. It shreds
what sunlight remains. The peace
of the grave intervenes,
sneaks into her sleep,
into the misery of all she is recalling,
the soldier who came to set her world on fire
and laughed as it spread.
She had enjoyed the old ways,
days of talking,
laughing, eating, men plaintively singing,
a flirt herself with a beau
on both arms. There's nothing left to know,
she would tell you, save for the prayers
she was made to repeat,
the remorse she felt afterward
when the horses fleeing
sounded loud as tanks on the cobblestones.

## One Day in History

1. Fifty hostages are randomly shot in reprisal near Rouen.
2. Nazis drive relentlessly into south Russia.
3. Soviet troops begin an offensive on the Karelian Isthmus.
4. A furious Himmler derides his army's high command.
5. Sugar is being shipped stateside from Hawaii.
6. Gas regulation begins after hoarding is widely reported.
7. Canada gets a final bill for a full draft.
8. Chinese advance on the Burma Road.
9. A boy is born in Memorial Hospital in Plainfield, New Jersey.
10. The Japanese broadcast the conquest of the Philippines.
11. General Sharp has surrendered on Mindanao.
12. A saboteur blows up the tower of Radio Paris near Bruges.
13. A proud Capaneus rages in vain against Thebes' gates.
14. A yawping paladin surmounts the ramparts of walled Carcassonne.

## Walter Benjamin

In fear for his life, he fled on a train from home to
safety in France. Deutschland would stand
for his sort no more. But Paris had fallen. Who
could have believed it? Nothing goes as planned.
He sits in a taverna, sipping a whiskey
at the foot of the Pyrenees. He has no passport,
no visa. He is trapped. All routes by sea
blockaded, the border closed, no honest court
to appeal to. It is past midnight. The barkeep
has long gone to bed, locking the shutters and doors.
There is no way back, ahead lies only the steep,
risky trek into Spain. Suicides are selfish as bores,
he knows. He smells a suckling pig being roasted
this late on an oven spit. How hungry he is. How exhausted.

**On Tragedy**

Wounded in bootcamp, a half-mad boy walks
awkwardly with a painful limp, retches all night.
Every morning, he cleans his guns. A widow who talks
to herself dresses in girlish smocks, is easily fright-
ened by birds that peck at the weeds in her garden.
A grizzled grandfather mocks his young grandson
for not trying, makes a sad face. Lashing out in a fren-
zy of hate, he rains down curse after curse on
a world filled with stupid people. Unshaven, dull-eyed,
a kid wearing Nazi garb roams the neighborhood
informing strangers his girl friend's just died,
his windowsills littered for weeks with rotting food.
You want to speak of tragedy. How at the end of the play you cried
for the great ones ruined. Look at us. Too much is made of magnitude.

## Home Front

June-bright jonquils.  A shallow creek
banked with red clay.
Dogwood tangled in ivy.
Two cardinals scrapping with a blue jay.

Dew-wet high grass.  Chipmunks,
squirrels the rust colors of pine
bark.  Bony-fingered
roots.  A No Trespassing sign used as a target.

An early June thunderstorm is on its way.
Tadpoles, newts, minnows
pink and silvery
in a green pond.  Bat-black grackles and crows.

He hears a throbbing sigh as puzzling as silence,
as his heartbeat at night
when he can't sleep.
Some sorrow far away, muted and white.

Clouds drift by gray and mottled,
the morning's rain-
soaked newspaper
tossed short of the porch, the pain

he knows, has seen on the front page
of his father dying,
the beach unreached, bodies
bobbing beside his in Normandy's tides.  Trying

not to cry, the boy becomes his loss of him, cold, clashing
waves roaring over him under sooty skies,
a brown sun, the din of guns, crashing
waves, thousands drowning near him short of the littered shore.

### Numbers Sanctify, My Good Fellow!

The fields lie fallow because of the lack of workers.
All the village's horses have been requisitioned.
The milk tastes of garlic. Deserters, shirkers,
they sneer. No wonder the boy is being questioned.
He can't go back. He begs them. He had been tied to the wire
between the lines in punishment for
refusing a mad captain's orders. The world is on fire,
isn't it? Isn't it? No wonder he shakes. He can't take it anymore.
Coward. Weak. No moral fiber
to him, they shout. It's over
for him, make no mistake
about it. No name on the village square's memor-
ial. No plaque to his memory anywhere. Was his death not murder?

Lorries' wheels clacking down a deserted street
in front of the burning courthouse. The bombardment continues in
the desolate park. Whizbangs. Tanks. The painful retreat
of men crawling out of trenches, dropping into gutters. The constant din.
The maddening despair of its never ending,
of never seeing another sunrise, sunset,
and everyone pretending
they will survive like the larks that persist in singing over
destitution, perched in trees too blasted by war
to bear leaves any longer till all the birds disappear
too into the smoky air and are no more. Let
it go. The fear of dying. The fear
of being forgotten, unhoused, just a number,
a cipher, one of the millions their kind killed. Were their deaths not murder?

## A Border Trilogy

### 1.

A shallow, serpentine river. A fence
twice taller than he is. A wall bolstered by
steel trusses. He makes what sense
he can of it. Understands why,
when the cops showed, he ran
so fast. A scene in a black and white movie.
A grainy gray desert. A long scan
toward the border. A man in jeans, too far away to see,

trying to slip
across, to find
a gap in the fence to squeeze through
after a harrowing trip,
to have left behind
his past too violent to view.

### 2.

He huddles in a makeshift camp. Crouches in a cage.
Sleeps on cement by a chain link fence. Iron bars
seal windows and doors. Guards rage
against him, deride his mysterious patience. Hours
pass slow as years as he waits. Who bled into the Rio Grande
to reach this place, to be free,
not afraid
of the world, what it has made

of him, his mask-like face
less scary than what he hides behind it:
the wild,
dead space
opening wider between him and us, desolate as the pit
he dug in the desert to bury his child.

*3.*

Steel dust, rust
flakes, the taste
of dread, metallic waste
on your tongue, the brute, iron just-
ice of metaphysical fences,
walls, a strict border,
the laws you succumb to, the senses
you suppress for a life more orderly and better.

A man is crossing mountain
passes, drought-dry arroyos,
fiery Sonoran
deserts he has trekked through before. No rain
is in store. No moral succor. No compassion. I pose
you the nation's oldest question. How did hope turn into a prison?

**Migrant**

Talking of going home, returning. Hungry,
thirsty, moved from camp
to camp. Dreams of see-
ing our mountains again. A moon like an oil lamp.
Painted walls, clothes dyed blood
crimson, turquoise, parrot green. Our river's
flood-
ed, churning waters.

The brown feathers of a chachalaca. Yellow
butterflies, black butterflies. Beads
hanging in doorways, sparkling. A meadow
in springtime, weeds
flowering like a garden. An iguana,
sunning on a rock, a sign of good luck our last day,

the sun at dawn like a girl filling
a window with light,
Mayan flutes, pipes, drums playing
in our heads
laments for the empty beds
left behind, the last sight
of friends picking guava, mangos, bananas for us to eat
on the way while a rooster crowed protesting the heat,

the dangers of our go-
ing, our distressed faces,
as we low-
ered bucket after bucket into the village well, tasting traces
of iron in the water,
of the blood of those gangs slaughtered more brutal than a war.

**A Mother and Her Son**

A mother's love for her child must be cease-
less even when it is not enough
to save him, no peace
from the grueling, tough
journey. Is a man a snake
that eats its own kind? Last night,
her boy fell sick. Why did they take
him away? She spies chainlink, barbed wire, floodlight.

Poisonous spiders, scorpions, scary trails, crumbling pyramids,
she and her son
struggling through jungle alone, in the desert his eyelids
encrusted with sand. Lying on the cement floor of the prison,
she stares out a barred window,
sees nothing. Sees Sky. Sees Texas. Sees Estuardo.

**Tikal**

The rainforest asleep, possessed by night,
by vine-entangled kapok,
strangled mahogany,

limestone monuments crumbled
into ruins, volcanic peaks,
basalt heads,

spider monkeys, howler monkeys, harpy eagles,
toucans, macaws, guans, ocelots,
cougars, leaf-eating

ants' scissors jaws, nightmares
of King Great-Jaguar-Paw,
of a blue painted

priest with his flint knife extracting
a beating heart spew-
ing red, its spasms

grasping for life, a body with an ax-event
glyph carved on it, its head
a ball for a game

to be played by victors at the foot
of the temple at Tikal
while I, tied to a tree,

weakened by hunger, abductee, I too
like the rainforest am unable
to awaken before the last blow falls.

## A Reliquary for Juan Carlos

Discovered in the desert
    near the border half-buried,
a small rock gleaming
    like a chunk of fool's
gold he had pocketed to rub
    for good luck
like bones stolen from
    a reliquary,
to stroke reverently like
    the retablo
hanging in his village's
    adobe church
painted on cracked wood
    in the colors of earth
and the insects and flowers
    in the grounds of
the cemetery where before he migrated
    he found sunglasses,
three centavos, a denim cap
    with a brim, a working
compass. All treasures. Each
    a sign of Jesús' help.
Juan Carlos winces, shivers from the pain
    of splinters, sharper
than the thorns a Coyote forced
    under his fingernails
two days ago. Recalls what
    the padre said to him
before he left on the overpacked
    truck. To be sure
to pray along the way thankful
    for the suffering
the Lord bore for him, what he paid
    for him to be smuggled
across the border, a small boy alone,
    trusting in paradise.

**Alejandro Saves Himself from Drowning**

Yesterday, a teenager almost drowned at Ocean Beach,
a tall boy from a village in Guerrero.
He had been playing with his cousin
in the surf, teaching
him how to swim
when a wave's battering blow
knocked him over
into the cold water
where a riptide dragged him out to sea
as his little sister
and his mother
were building sandcastles by
tide's edge. The girl looked up, saw
her cousin flailing in the undertow,
screamed at her mother. The two of them
rushed to him,
hauled him from the ocean
even as Alejandro,
strong boy from Guerrero,
not fighting the currents dragging him
further from the coastline,
swam north until he could safely
bodysurf to shore
and out of danger
to stand safely seaside
as if he hadn't been frightened,
scared to death,
the cocky boy,
I was told later,
who had dared
the guards at the border
to try to stop him, who had almost died
crossing it, helping his older brothers, twice in one night.

## Lawrence's Plumed Serpent

Lawrence's half-crazed
    fantasy of Mexico,
its subterranean oneiric memory
    of a primitive earth
unfettered by the sins of civilization
    like Lowry or Olson
after him seeking in the sacred darkness
    of caves in the Yucatan,
the secrets hidden in them,
    in the jungle, the knowledge
of terrifying, ravaging jaguar carvings,
    colossal scowling Olmec heads,
of Aztec priests shedding blood
    as the sun set
upon Tenoctitlan so that great city
    might survive to rise
from deep within the underland
    of reason
like the bloodied faces of the Aztec's
    death-drunk gods
whose return Lawrence desperately
    awaited as he lay dying.
I am trying to understand why so often
    violence embraces violence
whenever Western minds succumb to
    the enemies of the Enlightenment
as if they had been dispossessed
    by it of meaning,
Lawrence dreaming of becoming
    in his novel
Quetzacotl-the-Christ
    maddened by
his passion, undone by its victory.

IV

# Canticum Sacrum

Dawn mist rises off the canals. A man dons silk breeches. By the silvery sea,
a flower girl yawns. As part of the pageantry, ships display their brightest flags.
The basilica is a sunlit gold. A chalk-drawn horizon. Feathery clouds, white as ivory.
A light soft as candles'. A flock of red-throated loons that zigzags
over a lagoon. A young girl is beseeching her father to forgive
her lover, the old man crimson-faced, pocked, keen on revenge, though bound
by love to pardon her. It is Carnival. Masquerades. Who would not want to live
in this baroque opera of a city? The sun at its zenith and San Marco crowned.

Elaborate Greek, Byzantine mosaics, vaulting nave, dome, bell tower
all enflamed, a fountain spouting water from twin lions' mouths in Cannaregio.
To honor Pound's and Stravinsky's graves in San Michele, let us cross the water
in a gondola by sight of its cypress trees. Let us go there in the warm glow
of the aftermath of a sunset red as the wine we pour for them in duty, in obeisance
onto their marble slabs. Let us hear their sacred songs. Let us bow to God in Venice

## Murillo's After the Flagellation of Christ

On hands and knees, he grapples for or grabs at his dirty, rumpled cloak
on the mud floor, his hair and beard knotted, sweaty,
his body gashed, gouged by nettles and whips. Fresh blood is soak-
ing his loin cloth, his back, thighs scarlet as a rash that is growing darkly
more scab-like as it spreads. He would hide his nakedness.
He would keep his eyes shut as if blinded. The ropes that lashed and beat
him dangle from a column. The room is a torture chamber for confes-
sions. A tomb slashed out of rock where grief never ends, torment is complete.

His is a metaphysical pain born of whips and thorns. Or a strange grace. Their feet
like dancers, weighty, arched to float skyward despite their muscularity,
their garments thistle blue, rose rust, two angels gaze
down upon him less in human horror than mystified by
what he has had to endure, as if it does not faze
them quite, winged as they are, to have witnessed how easily flesh suffers defeat.

Witnesses detached as his father is, one might say, who must stare down
from somewhere impossible to behold. Look. Look anyplace around you.
In forests or farmlands. On the sea. In every village, town,
or city. Consider the ordinary sorrows all people daily suffer through.
A mother in the bedroom where her dying son sleeps, so dear
to her she cannot bear it. An old man in his jail cell slow-
ly fading away. I should tell you of a friend lying on a gurney long ago,
filthy as Lazarus, lacerated by sores, his sight, coming back, brightened by fear

## Lear's Fool

His part of the play is over. Before dawn, helpless, wandering
deserted city streets, mumbling
to himself, crying out against the dark something
unspeakable, not quite raving, more like despair,
"Friends, friends," he begs, pleading to air,
a streetlight hurting his eyes as a car drives by, trying not to hit him,
maneuvering across the median,
the driver screaming at him, he hollering
back mocking his voice, though phlegm
caught in his throat chokes him, strangles the sound. Wait. A gold ring
surrounds the moon. Watch him catch it in his finger. Or perhaps it is a diadem
for him to wear in his hair like a crown–prancing,
dancing, finally happy, my darling, disappearing
into his rôle of the king's last truly sane companion.

## Fryderyk

Like whirlwinds, storms of notes
blowing through his mind,
nighttime frightens the boy,
sun fast sinking,
a sad half rainbow
arcing westward
in the aching aftermath
of winter rains,
mortality lying
in wait, a wolf
in the White Forest,
like an army besieging
Warsaw's gates,
Poland's past in its wayward violence.

Wood warbler, keeper
of wilderness's secrets.
Or wagtails, waxwings,
thrushes spirited
by chance of wind.
A hearth fire's sparks flying
toward smoke-gray clouds
in an ember-red sky.
Or is it a nocturne like the one
he is writing, smoldering like coal,
transforming desire
into immortal things,
like day's passage
into sunset's brightest ashes.

**February 13, 1883**

Edelweiss, chamomile, alpine roses. Perfumes of favored flowers. Incense
burning from a goddess' pyre. The campanile, bell towers shadow
children playing in the basilica's square. Silence
broken only by tides lapping against the palazzo, a rower
singing. Mirroring the noon sun, the Adriatic is blanched, scalded, white
as snow on meadows. How right
life appears as he leaves it. Canals take fire, water burns, as his eyesight
dims. His wife's Buddha smile, his hands' hectic flush, day's waxen light.

It is an embarkation. A gondolier begins his trip across the Styx.
Go, not in penance
for faults but with a little gold, a few lire to hear his songs. All music's
intended for the dying, composed
for those who would sing it, even if the keys must be transposed
to suit their voices like Bach for a choir of boys he once heard in Venice.

## J. M. W. Turner

A brisk, crackling late June wind, sunset on an evening
so prolonged it stays a golden red
for over an hour, gilding
the air, brightening the white feathers of the gulls gliding over head
to a jewel-like amber. The bluffs at Land's
End blaze. The cliffs behind me, by twilight's intensity,
gleam like slabs of burnished steel mirroring a fire. Who understands
this beauty understands God. The sea
is a lotus-blue, the waves, where they peak, yellow-tinted,
the sand blowing across the beach like pollen
drifting in early spring breezes. A raven
struts on driftwood, black as a priest. Look. A day dies prestidigitated
by light into the glow from the rose windows of a cathedral,
sky and earth and you and all.

# Kafka

Though bottom up, a crab attacks with its claws and legs,
gulls, ravens hungrily pecking at it
as its twitching body begs
for a sort of mercy, a pit
in its belly already slit open by a crow's
sharp beak.
A little girl prods it with a stick, who knows why,
out of curiosity, I suppose,
then turns it over as if try-
ing to encourage it to sneak
away, save itself, crawl toward the sea
that at high tide had abandoned
it on the beach's black sand as if an ocean's enormity
could rectify what it had done by disobeying the law the Lord had commanded.

## À Jarry

An icy wind is rife with the stink of rotting leaves and everything
wasted as life slumps back toward winter. By an abandoned park,
workmen dig to expose frozen sewer lines that zigzag and swing
along a twisting road. The wind blows wilder. Smoldering clouds darken.
A man who wears a greatcoat sways on his feet as a stark,
last ray of light breaks through. Horns blare news of no noon coming
as a test of the warning system. Lying half buried in a ditch, a styrofoam cup
is doing its best to drown in the ordure. The tottering half-mad man picks it up.

Try not to panic, people. It's only politics. Yes, each day more rain falls
ever more heavily. Look how it soaks your clothing, too. Yes, he is dying.
So are you, aren't you? You were warned. The deluge is inevitable. Purifying.
He drinks from the cup. So would you if you felt as sick as he does. Who scrawls
his name with a finger in mud, forms a U like a rainbow's arc.
You knew Ubu. You loved him. Your long ruling king: killer, dung dealer, patriarch.

**Ferrara's Pasolini**

His is the poetry of catastrophe in an age of assassins.
A pink sand desert infinite as injustice
in which a plane crashes killing all on board. Who wins
their place in the halls of power? Vermin. Lice.
Pasolini is a Medea riven from a people of rites,
their lives made meaningful by the sun's cruelties.
He is a man crushed to death by a hustler, beaten by beachside nights
for a lust he will neither deny nor betray, for a need greater than the sea's.

Ninetto is his sole Epiphany, his white hair still curly as a boy's.
Gaze back on earth with him, Pier Paolo. See
what he sees. How its pain, its happiness, sorrows, joys
belong to the oldest gods of tragedy.
The afterlife of art is what it saves from life by looking. Cinema. The eyes
it opens to the world's brief splendors before God closes the doors to paradise.

## The Movie Version

There is nothing like this in the world, nothing at all, you say,
the Riviera beach we stroll on like the movie version crowded with beautiful
boys and girls, sailors, thousands of tourists, a few locals
enticed to join them by a balmy, sensuous late July Saturday,
the water warm, the waves peaceful, a carved-wood-white perfect seagull
gliding over children playing with gaily colored beach balls
in the shallow water, women rubbing lotion on their thighs, the bay
a perfect Saint-Tropez blue, a Monet painting. Nothing, you say. Nothing more fine
    and terrible.

Six thousand miles west, four decades after, at dawn in August, the Pacific is fogged in.
There is a three day multi-stage concert underway in Golden Gate Park.
Only a thinning slip of the coastline is visible, the waves roaring
louder than winds in a winter storm. By noon, the bands' rousing din
will fill the neighborhood. Nothing more terrible than this, you said, nothing
more fine, like the last show before it closes in our favorite movie theater the moment
    it goes dark.

## Out of the Past

Sailing westward, storm clouds slowly dissolve, pale
as snow melting on stones,
lustrous as pewter or polished tin. A dead fin whale
lies on the beach. Joe's drone's
buzzing over head, snapping photos.
China bound, a cargo ship looks pencilled in,
added to a film noir scene, its soft light and ominous shadows
creating contrasting tonalities: hazy rain, a veil of clouds, whale skin.

A giant creature of God lies dead on the beach, mottled gray,
bleached gray, the gray of faded rubber,
driftwood that has floated for years in seawater,
sun-dulled tar, or a wet asphalt highway.
By the dunes, an excavator waits to dig a grave for it near where, in the thirties,
gangsters drive to late at night, ordered to ditch the bodies.

## Linda's Kore

Perhaps her poems have fulfilled her dreams,
her longings after all and so have become the poet
as much as she who wrote them. Perhaps
they have shown her readers what life meant
her to become: the prayers that survive her.
In them, deer still nip at her precious small breasts
on a hill in west Marin. A yearling nibbles
her golden hair. Though her horse has trotted
away, its beauty quiets her soul. She feels as free
as the love-struck girl she was on Santorini. As unable to stay.

What do her poems revive? The sea. Flayed snakes
seeking dark trees. Whatever might save a spirit
from grief. Why let it all go? Why despair of passion?
Words, images tasting of ripe melons, redolent
of does roaming in woods, shiny as the shawls
of black clad widows washing clothes on rocks,
fated as salmon swimming upstream to spawn.
She has shut her windows to the city's intrusions,
to whatever would make her forget, refuse
her her faith in words' capacity to restore sanctified things.

Sacred as a bowl of brown rice sprinkled with sesame
seeds and soy sauce. Small pleasures that suffice
to remind her, even after she has set her pen
aside for good, what a poem can be when worthy
of the permanent hurt she feels, the wound
of perpetual mourning, the pain of final
things. Yet graced as well with happiness, sudden
laughter like Jack's child-like sighing with delight
over her body in the aftermath of their ecstasy.
Why let mortality obscure either sun or its shadows?

Rejoice in the good you are given. Life sweet as honeyed
almonds, lemon cakes gently frosted.
Moments precious as island breezes, heron fishing in a lake,
fern fronds at twilight, swallows in flight,
her own bright nakedness while bathing under
a moonlight that shines with the same soft
radiance through paneless windows onto the bed
where she and Jack made love each night.
Why permit life, like a man, to shut its doors
on her, lock her in a closet, leaving no way out as he prowls?

Old women must still thresh in the valley east
of the mountain in Paros where she found
the terra-cotta shard of a kore, her kore,
whom she believed to be holier than
Aphrodite, the fragments, head, arms, torso,
she had dug up with her fingers, clawed
for deep into the ground, the girl's headband
wound round the plaited strands of her hair.
She could have watched them forever: the crane
and two white-eyed gulls flying above the olive grove.

Bound to the myth, I say, Let waves shift sand and pebbles
on Kolymbithres' fossil-like granite beach
while the sun-bright sea, dazzling at sunrise,
answers her prayers. Let her glance up at the kore
resting on her shelf in her apartment. What
beauty, Semele-like, has set it on fire today?
She listens intently to the women of the chorus
chanting of the water-bearer, the threnody
poems learn to sing after their poet has died. Untimely
Semele who for her passion burned with the knowledge of god.

## Parade

*1.*

Codes he learns. Yellow on Thursdays, blue on Mondays.
Harsh laws. Deviants beaten, purged, imprisoned.
Hide the truth. Lie. Keep silent. The roles he plays.
Nothing to brag of except to say later: See. I survived.

His first night in a gay bar, everyone, everything
so beautiful he stays in Frisco. The joy of it, the freedom.
Tricks. Boyfriends. Parties. No one refusing
him happiness. No one calling him names. He is home.

Naked boys on beaches, in baths, back rooms.
He takes a lover or two to get through winters.
Summer orgies in Laguna, on Fire Island. He assumes
it will last. Parades. Marches. Dancing in bars.

Then the rumors start, grim phone calls. The list
he keeps of names of men he knew, embraced,
screwed, hugged the morning after, kissed
goodbye without needing to say why. Their bodies wasted.

*2.*

Before dawn, blurred by the steam while he shaved,
he caught Carlo's face in the mirror. His black hair.
His dark eyes flecked gold and copper. Carlo had saved
him. Now he is lost, like someone gone missing. Despair,

a gap in his soul, a hole bored into him, expanding,
black, implacable. The half-empty bed, year
after year. His clothes he kept but couldn't wear
himself. A bare chair, an unset place at table. A ring.

Sunday is his last parade. He has grown old, scared
of streets packed for a party. Long ago, he dared
to march at the start of the line, holding the banner.
Now Carlo, others must take his place, that honor,

ghosts of the moment returning in the failure of solace,
silently beckoning as they quicken the pace
ahead of the rest of the marchers, the paraders
following as they once pursued hoped for boyfriends and lovers.

**Curricula**

Collegiate Gothic dorms, classrooms, fraternities
built from local dolomite.  Others of brick, smoke-
blackened by punitive winters.  A few white New England
clapboard houses with wooden Doric columns, wrapped porches.

A Victorian mock mini-castle with a spired mimic
turret, romantic as a Scott novel.  A cottage,
its oldest building, preserved as a relic for
secret meetings by select societies.  Wide swards

of grass carefully tended for soccer and lacrosse,
a golf course, quads' rolled lawns, a football field
with its bleachers seating no more than two hundred,
a stadium in miniature on a campus so carefully composed

it could be read like a lyric poem articulated by
glens, meadows, and haunted woods.  A hill's steep
descent to village taverns, the climb back up sobering.
A three story chapel, lead paned windows, clocks

and chimes in its steeple marking lives and classes,
the passage of time as the college chose to
display it, an orderly place safe for becoming
well-read, thoughtful gentlemen, the essential

texts needed for inherited tasks.  Homer, the Bible,
Shakespeare, Milton, Wordsworth, Conrad.  Greek, Latin,
German, French, Spanish.  Philosophy.  The core
sciences.  Math.  The history of the world offered

in four years to us living outside it.  Choral singing, theater.
(Shakespeare, Jonson, Beaumont and Fletcher,
Beckett, Christopher Fry.)  Houses parties, days and nights
consumed by beer or scotch or stingers.  Autumn as written

or inspired by Keats, sensuous, melancholy, enflamed
by the heat of its colors.  Winter snows piling up to
second stories, drifts white as seas stilled by moonlight.
Spring arriving tardily, too late, delayed like a love letter

lost in the mail until suddenly it appears, opening itself
in your hands, it seems, its words more joyous than you
might have written yourself, more surprising. And you delight
in it, in every spring, despite how briefly each stays faithful.

For tragedy, our teachers if challenged might intimate, belongs to chaos,
the dark beyond learning's borders they have spared us from,
like Renaissance humanists saving the past from its violence,
as Mattingly taught us, by restoring its ancient books and languages.

How could I not believe as I did, as knowledge used to, that life
becomes comprehensible, even beautiful if you read enough
and write about it with humility? We were assured change was
an illusion if seen through the timeless. If we'd been deceived, so be it.

Years after, I still owe a debt to what some now call lies. I am trying to remember,
my long lost friend, how true life looked the March night we held gloveless
hands while crossing a bridge in Root Glen, the creek iced over as together
we quoted Coleridge, the hornèd moon with one bright star within the nether tip.

V

## Ground Fog

Flying toward the beach, plovers, sandpipers darken into carved
birds, stone or driftwood figures shadowing dunes.
A foggy morning. Unobserved,
he studies the houses around him, lit by moon's
descent, where his neighbors lie dreaming. A thick mist
gathers before first light,
floating like dust in a slight breeze, tiny chips of cry-
stal dancing in the air. All is good. All is right.

He waits until the sun rises to bless
the eastern hills, lets his mind roam
where it will. Time appears
suspended, a lovely, hazy dawn that brings him to confess-
ion. He has lived for fifty years
in a beautiful place. In a radiance of expectation, the hope that feels like home.

# Childhood Scenes

   *1.* Phantom Empire, 1948

Saturday mornings, I watched episodes of Phantom Empire,
serial reruns from the thirties shown on TV. Thousands of feet
underground, its world hides dire
prophecies from those who live above, sheet-
hooded warriors dressed like Ku Klux Klan
men, denizens of an antediluvian
underground city, Mu, violent
and cruel, its assaults on the innocent
unrelenting, its robots,
ray guns, mine-deep elevator
in its tight iron shaft, radium powers, bombs and loud gunshots,
each caped, terrifying Thunder Rider,
and Queen Tika, nightmarish ruler, destroyer
of rest, night's tyrant, all rising to scare me like rumors I hear spreading of another war.

   *2.* A Gift for My Father, 1950

It is December dark at five o'clock after the kid's matinee. Tomorrow
is my father's birthday. He'll turn forty-five. I am eight. What to buy
him with little money? I've already spent my allowance, must borrow
a dollar from my best friend Teddy. I wonder if I could lie,
should say I forgot the date, make up some excuse. But I find
in a hardware store open late a finger-sized flashlight on a chain
with two batteries included. It might do, be gift enough, a remind-
er of the night last month when the electricity failed. I had lain
in bed after, uneasy in my room listening to the storm growing more
and more violent until my father walked in to comfort me holding two candles
that smelled like the incense burnt during communion at church. Never before
had he looked so ghostly pale, his face in shadows, lined with wrinkles,
old as his own father. I am a boy learning new fears. With my quarter and Teddy's
dollar, I buy the plastic flashlight. Will it let him love me better, longer? Will it please?

   *3.* The Wizard of Oz, 1951

Oz terrifies me. The Munchkins. The Wicked Witch of the West
piteously dying, her knife-sharp nose, chartreuse face,
claw-like fingers, black wardrobe and hat like the rest
of her melting, melting in her death throes. It's a nightmarish place.
Plastic hothouse daisies, dahlias, roses in garish billboard
neon colors. Scarecrow, Tin Man, Lion poisoned, dozing

off, perishing in snow as sands in an hour glass record
to the second the moment of Dorothy's doom. Broomsticks like flaming
wicks. Shrunken-head faces of a costumed monkey army. Snake-
like slithering yellow brick roads, bleeding trees, painted streams—
all intensified by a horror comic's vividness. An on-the-take
phony pitchman carnival huckster, it proves, is manipulating my dreams.
Merry-go-round colored pastel horses. Crushing portcullises. They say, Come
back to us, Son. We have no magic shoes for you to wear. We promise no way home.

### 4. At the Museum of Natural History with My Father, 1953

A Mesoamerican show in Manhattan. A huge basalt head
gouged, pitted, split, decapitated.
Women's snarling lips. Babies' faces distorted
by rage. Stone chips. Polished votive axes. Jade,
turquoise decorated jaguar amulets, jewelry, fancy masked
dolls retrieved from tombs. Undeciphered X's like scratches on a stone
stele. A little boy carved from wood, pliable as wax, asked
me with his artful mournful eyes if I might comfort his lone-
liness. I wished I could. What gods would make him suffer
so? I must have gasped. My father,
understanding, grabbed my hand, said
what he had never
told me before, "What has stayed
with me all my life was a man I heard beating his son as if he knew no better."

### 5. Nights of the Living Dead, 1954

I believed boys like me did turn into a zombie,
into the undead, if fantasy,
dreams, movies, TV
I didn't need to see
but watched anyway told me the bitter truth. Each Saturday,
I mow my father's lawn, trim
the trees. Finished with chores, I play
by the lake alone until the light becomes dim
enough for me safely to return home.
The grass I have cut is smooth, clean
as a putting green, rich loam
and mulch below it. Kids are sometimes mean
to me, my father easily angered. The walking dead. I sit up straighter the better
to see, a pubescent boy, trying to learn what bodily nightmares might plague him later.

*6.* Forsyth County Fair, 1955

We say we go for the rides, Ken and I, the treats. But, no. We miss
them on purpose for the tattooed men. Freak shows.
Scarred, fat women naked in caravans. A geek kiss-
ing the beak of a chick he'll swallow for money. Embryos,
fetuses pickled in jars displayed in a circus tent. Too young,
forbidden to enter, we snuck in, saw—
bewildered, disgusted, I suppose—their wrinkled faces, dungcolored
flesh, each tiny hand a claw
with a pigmy monkey's clenched grip, tightly
closed eyes, the babies never to be,
what no one at our age need ever see,
reality, life's fragility and suffering, child, parent, so easily
loosed, untethered from any protection of home, the free-
dom from fear we believed was our due when we were just born lucky.

*7.* The Last Sleepover, 1956

Southern summer nighttime swelter. Ken's dormer window
looked out toward woods we had hiked in all day,
his mother's camellia garden, a rolling green meadow.
He pushed his twin beds closer, the bla-
zing heat in the room cooled by an incoming breeze
that fanned us both, tightly pressed together. It was past time for sleep.
We stripped to our briefs. Lay back on the sheets. Please,
he said, and crossed the border that was meant to keep
us apart. A quiet touching. Some kissing. Then him deep inside me until it was over.
It was nothing to break our friendship for after,
though, both virgins before, we had nothing to measure
its importance by. Nothing had changed
between us, it seemed. Only an unspoken pleasure
we never repeated. The secret dreams our bodies had exchanged.

*8.* An Angry Argument, 1958

I sit on a curb. It is dark. No streetlights are permitted
in our neighborhood. My mind is wander-
ing far from home. In his slippers, pajamas, robe, my father
calls to me where I hide in shadows. I have just said
something cruel to him. Invisible as night,
I imagine myself racing past the iron
gate and a lawn, meticulously shorn and tended

as a formal garden. Back in my room, a light
wind whistles through a loose pane. I am not alone.
Listen. The key is in the lock. The latch clicks. The door
opens. My father walks in. Why do I retreat from him more
in my imagination? He places his hand on my shoulder.
I am trying not to tremble or sob. I am working hard to gather
thoughts, to make sense of a dream. To hear, "My son." To be loved beyond reason.

# A Boy's Secret Garden

A ladder-high brick wall, a stream rippling near it, a locked gate, boxwood maze, stickseed burs clinging to his pants and jacket, plush grass, trellised vines, white lattice work that surrounds a stone well at the center of a garden the boy would linger in forever, vowed to stay to the end of the story he tells himself, another boy whispering him his secret, his wish never to leave there either, who touches his arm, brushes his hair with his fingers, who, to embrace him, leaps out of a wicker chair in the whitewashed, arabesque gazebo and stares at his face as if it were his own he saw in the mirror of the well's brown waters.

No words. A sweetly warm spring rain drizzles on them until the sun sneaks through weakened clouds. Perched in a cypress tree, two jays berate the late May Carolina heat, magnolia's and scotch broom's perfumes thickening the air, heavy as mist, gardenia's rust-lipped petals floating freely as feathers spiraling down. Spiky spruce needles, chips of oak bark sail on the stream like paper boats on their way to places distant from home and harbor.

Imagine a boy's quickening desires, how they yearn for his secret garden needing no key to unlock its gate, the door he enters it by, a garden that welcomes him in it, the ferns and soft grass he would lie on with his friend while they listen to Sunday church bells resounding before dying sweetly faraway.

Imagine two boys, eleven or twelve, real or not, who can say?, basking under an endless sun until twilight lets descend upon them its protective shadows, shaded woods, pine, cypress, hickory, spruce, every tree one by one darkening, gathered by a night that, as upon a river, casts a viridescent glow that intensifies the flowers to a sharp chartreuse while a mantis devours a fluttering milk white anise butterfly as if its hunger is meant as a sign to say it is time to return to reality.

In the aftermath of youth, do old men recall the green things that long ago foretold a paradise a lifetime could not prove was false? Fresh leaves sparkling like jade glistening. Winged seeds drifting, lifted higher by evening's careful breezes. White, silvery threads of dandelions shimmering as brightly as the sunlit dew dawn spreads over boxwood, lawn, and meadow. Newer seeds after they have fallen taking on the verdant hue of the grass and vines, the foliage, the mossy soil of a storied pastoral childhood the boy believed was true.

Suppose it were so, the future like a garden I mean, green lynx spiders, milkweed stalks, emerald days, lilies by creeks, all the green world you did not mean to leave remembering for you forever.

## First Communion

A winter chill in the air. Pouring down
on fresh snow,
the sun

slowly melts the crust, exposing
a woodchuck pelt
rotting

at the edge of the forest. On his way
to his first communion,
a boy spots it,

grabs it, lifts it skyward like a trophy. Dead
white maggots cling to it, white
as a choir boy's surplice.

He'd like to explore an underground cave
on his own some day, be
a spelunker,

listen to stalactites dripping, dripping
like icicles off trees.
Snow on snow

piled beside the roadway where he walks.
Secure your locks. Close
all shutters.

I'm a gay boy. Let night fall black as cinders.
He lives like a boarder within
his own home,

his heart resounding, beating harder whenever
he spies the kid
who will kneel

beside him at the communion rail. Air he
can't bear to breathe,
brittle,

cold as his mind grows at thoughts
of God.  Stay away, Lord.
Don't knock

on my door.  No more catechism.
I won't let you in.
Last night

he dreamed of albino fish, translucent, eyeless,
swimming in the bottomless
pool of the cave

nothing can save him from.  His sins.
No more delaying.  He walks on,
just a few more blocks

to his church where his family joins him.
Snow on more snow.  Life
upstate,

its shadeless glow.  Heaven should be
invisible, no need
to confess

to anyone, no altar cross, blinding as the sun,
no desire,
no boys

he is tempted to stare at.  No ice on fire.
No eucharist.  No
Joey's blue eyes.

## Altar Boys

For a moment this morning, he feared he had forgotten
his name, though not the Sundays they were acolytes together,
lighting candles, swinging incense, gen-
uflecting, carrying trays of wine and the host to Pastor.

Once, as they changed into their robes, he had caught his stares
and blushed at what both feared to let go any further.
Rick. It was Richard Carlson. The old man has lived the life of a wanderer,
searching for all he had lost along with his childhood prayers.

He can't find in his messy desk the only photograph
of him he had saved. To forget is like a sleepless night
spent past dreaming, isn't it?. The half-remembered like a persecutor.

He has lost Rick's picture. Why can't he quit looking for it? He would laugh
at himself if he could. Mock his adolescent faith. The sight
of him and Rick flush-faced, kneeling, smiling at each other across the altar.

## Listening to Ives with Bob at Ojai

*1.*

The sun rises over a brightening valley, a sleepy sun, bedded in feathery pillows of clouds. Dawn is rust-colored, dusted with red. It is the first weekend in June. Paul Zukovsky and Gilbert Kalish are rehearsing Ives' Violin Sonatas in Ojai's bandshell beneath its arching, centuries' old sycamore.

They have woken the insects, clicking, chattering, twittering, clacking to the largo of the Fourth Sonata for Violin and Piano with its sad, scrapbook reminiscences of times long past.

Just above where Bob and I lie on the lawn, a thrush warbles to it like a Chinese flute, its song wafting through softly billowing breezes that ruffle its tan and ochre feathers.

*2.*

Years ago, perhaps some seven or eight years before Ives composed the sonata he entitled "Children's Day at the Camp Meeting," an elderly woman wakes at first light in the bare bedroom of the cold stone home her husband built for her by a pond in a village in western Connecticut, a frail, lonely widow who is staring out her window at a garden a next door neighbor tends for her, a sad woman who will not forget her boy killed forty years before in the Battle of the Wilderness, the loss she survives only by recalling all she has saved of her love for him.

I imagine her as I listen again in memory because I am trying to find a way of saying what hearing Ives' music meant to Bob and me just after dawn one Sunday in Ojai. So tell you about it in a story that might even be true.

*3.*

Perhaps, however rarely, what we mean by love might be an image in which what we once experienced is recovered from scraps of time. Ojai might be one of those tales, Bob's and mine. Insects chittering. Tree frogs croaking. Birds singing. One thrush in particular I recall sweetly warbling while Paul Zukovsky and Gilbert Kalish practiced Ives for their performance hours later.

All of it, all Bob and I hear together on an early June morning, still sleepy from last night's love making, lying stretched out on the grass in Libbey Park near the bandshell staring up at its sycamore while listening to Ives, all of it a moment in our lives over forty years ago gathered, recollected perhaps too easily into one music I attend to now with its late-life meaning.

Which is this. Which I'll try to state plainly. There is a spirit that dwells deep down in things that sometimes strangely continues to sing of what just might last forever.

# Rice Wine

*1.*

The crane of the heart flies to the moon
and is lost in its light,
Wei Ying-wu wrote.

Stalking in reeds by the lake, moon-startled
and white, two herons
drink sorrows.

A crane flies in silence to a waning moon in his poem,
flies into quiet. I stare at a lake
and tall reeds' shadows.

There is a light that divides day from night,
like flawed yellow jade
the color of your hair.

It is a drunken monk, a spiritual fool Wei Ying-wu
writes about who sees a crane
flying to the moon

and imagines it to be a fish whose silvery scales
glitter star-like in the pond
he dives into.

*2.*

I met you shortly after you returned from two years
fighting in Vietnam. There is an unnamed
season in Brown County,

you said, trying to describe your twenty four months
at war, as if early spring
and late fall were the same,

a season of perpetual waiting. While hiking in a gentle
Indiana fall rain, we stumbled upon a pond
so algae infested

it reminded you of the Nam you were wounded in, a bright
emerald jungle green, a tarnished copper's
acidic green, sickening to you.

Dry leaves, feverish as rotting trees lay scattered
on the ground around it.
You picked

fallen twigs off the autumn brittle grass to toss into
a crumpled trash can and kissed me
just that once.

3.

Wei writes of boats docked in a storm waiting
for clearer days to travel that might never
come his way again

and of a House of Pleasure lovely as a silk screen
he visits daily lest more tempestuous,
war-fraught times should follow,

bereft at heart because there is no rice wine the Emperor's
soldiers have left behind unspoiled
or undrunk.

## My Husband's Garden

Flowers the colors of cloisonné green butterflies, scarlet finches, blue
pheasants, like the rays of light stitched into a Chinese
silk gown we admired behind glass in the Asian Museum.

As dawn floods over the eastern hills, gilding clouds
a lambent gold, his garden's blossoms
are dappled by sunlight into hues motley and fragile as coral.

Dozens of stargazer lilies, their pink and white petals floating
in crystal bowls, glistering as if wet from dew,
sparkling like shells low tide reveals like jewels on the beach.

Content in his garden alone, Atticus cuts flowers for a vase,
prunes thorns off rose's stems, humming, smiling
like a child enchanted by magic, the wizardry of noon,

two aging men, fragile as flowers blooming despite the coming cold,
as the pungent scents of petals lingering in the breeze
long after they have fallen, as time slipping from our weakened fingers.

Love like a flower in the heart that opens at night,
nocturnal primroses, white lilies, moonflowers
budding, blossoming, flourishing, as old men might, better in the beautiful dark.

## Free Variations on Two Parables by Antonio Machado

*1.*

Stay steady and patient, my friend. Take keen note of the tide as it changes.
Wait as your boat in dry dock waits. Don't be overly eager
to return to the sea. Whoever in patience manages
to delay departure wins in the end since life lasts longer
than poetry which is only a game we like to play sometimes. But if life
should prove brief, as it often does, and the sea too risky for the dinghy
or rowboat you would escape in, remain patient despite whatever strife
troubles your days and old ways of believing. Don't go. Don't leave us. Be
hopeful since maybe poetry is what you stay here for, after all,
what you must live near,
by the sea.

*2.*

But God is not the same as the sea. God is of the sea he chooses to shine
on like moon upon water. It is where he appears, if he does, out of nowhere
like the white sails of a boat silently bound for an empty shoreline.
The sea is his bed, where he wakes up and, in spite of great cares,
falls asleep on sometimes, too. The sea he created is the sea that also bore
him like a mother, matrix of springtime and its storms. He is the creator
whose creatures fear they have created him, yet whose breath is their spirit
forever and ever. Have I made you, Lord, they wonder, as you with your spit
and clay made me? No. But adore him within you whom you've divined. The stream
of compassion, of love in its kindness, is a God who flows seaward like a dream
that passes from one heart into the night thoughts dreamed by another.

Oh Mother,
Father,
torrential rain
is fast
falling from clouds
that obscure you
from all our knowing.
If it must last,
if it must drown us,
let it mean something.

## Notes I Never Wrote to My Father

*1.*

You yelled at the bottom of the stairs each morning, shouted
"What are you doing up there? You're late. It's school time."
A Tuscaloosa mob rioting, hollering chants of "Kill her", led
by Klansmen, Russians crushing resisters in Poland. I'm
trying to remember what else. Young boys, younger than
I was, mere kids being tortured, murdered in Algeria. I'd seen
the photographs of them tied to posts with barbed wire. (Maybe, you said, a man
can stand only so much before cracking.) But old news isn't what I mean
to write you of, though history rhymes with our every act. Not asleep,
I lay on my bed pretending I couldn't hear your repeatedly shouting,
"Hurry up, I'm leaving," and, as if oblivious, returned to exciting
myself with fantasies of current crushes. I liked to think of my life as deep
in those days, but it wasn't. You were right to be impatient
the many occasions I made you wait. Profligate boy. In pursuit of the one sensation.

*2.*

Sprawled on a bench, almost luxuriating, a man in wine-soaked,
ripped, bedraggled clothes is feeding gulls and crows
from a box of sweet corn cereal. All humanity is yoked
to one another, you, no snob, cautioned me. Maybe the half-drunk man knows,
understands everything I know, too. Who can say? A white and blue windsurfer's sail
flies over the dunes like a lost balloon. A punk on a motorcycle
zooms past me, gunning his engine, nearly hitting an old lady. To fail
is the only crime, you assured me, the only sin that is allowed the reasonable
man. But you must try not to fall, Son. In sweats, pony tails tied with pink ribbons,
two girls jog around me. The bum shoves
flakes from the box into his mouth, chokes, wheezes until
he spits them out like vomit. Caritas. I have failed caritas. Religion's
such a strange and difficult thing, Father. The kindnesses, the loves
we might have given one another. Not the passionate clash of will against will.

*3.*

Perhaps, after all, it is solitude that made the world, yet left it undivided,
day, when you consider it, much like dark. Last night,
I watched a ground-hugging fog swallow a whitewashed
half-moon as if hungry, famished for its light,
an almost comic sight. This morning, mist hovers over our neighborhood,
sparing waking eyes a summer bright sunrise. I think of you dead,

yet still struggling to breathe. I have never understood
how you freed yourself from life so easily. "Sleep is my best friend," you said.
Sometimes I believe the heart begins and ends
in betrayal, how we delay say-
ing goodbye when it is long past time to say it.
I write you this note, admitting it cuts deep, rends
my heart as well, since what I say makes me look to be a liar. Father, pray
for me. Bless me, despite all I've kept hidden from you, the praise, the thanks I omit.

# VI

## After Sappho

### 1.

Mt. Tamalpais,
too green for Greece yet
god-lit,

a dream of a strange peace
on fire in the sunset
behind it,

a goat cart
in my ears as I watch
children play-

ing at the start
of evening, two boys catch-
ing in their hands the last light of day.

### 2.

Wind-, fog-drenched, not rain
but mist dazzling, cool-
ing late morning,

a beach where, see, again
boys like us in a tide pool
idly wading.

### 3.

Summer weather
in Carolina fifty five
years ago,

or today, here, where it is hotter,
less clear, alive
with tourists, no

thunderstorms mid-aft-
ernoon, no fireflies
at evening

as at twilight back home, we two laugh-
ing, counting how many, your sighs
more joyful than anything.

4.

Like wind to sails, blue
skies to sun, boys as young
as we, not yet men,

concealing nothing, yet not quite true
either, speechless, like a tongue
on fire with all it burns unspoken.

5.

Your skin after swimming like oil
on a naked wrestler
in heroic Greece,

youth unspoil-
ed by fear. The epic matter
of hair like gold fleece.

6.

Though no Sappho,
of course, I would pray
to the sea,

horizon, unbro-
ken sky, "May you stay
forever by me."

7.

Waves unerringly
roar, the Pacific I
walk beside

daily, ocean older than memory
now at its high-
est known tide,

a sea ancient as Homer's, no
less wild, vast, dan-
gerous to

voyage on, to be betrayed by: not you
but him, long ago, racing through rain
to someone new.

## A Medieval Manuscript of Job 2:9

An impoverished, untonsured, novice monk copies from scripture
a Latin he cannot understand, though committing few errors
so precise is his attention to the task, never lax, always sure
to reproduce every letter with exactitude. Cells' doors
close. It is Compline. He blows out his candle. To meditate
is like each stroke he must replicate on a page. Words
that feel like heaven almost. That unimaginable. Why hesitate?
He pauses, unfinished, unready to join others in prayer. Birds.
He misses most the flight of birds, he a child, a lost sickly child
without parents, abandoned, ill-prepared to survive the wild
world outside. The corridors are cold as icy water. Benedic
Deo et morere. What might the passage mean? A plaintive music
fills the chapel, the monks' low chanting. Go. Each sign you imitate, make
on a page, is like a bird on the wing, free to mean nothing, singing for the song's sake.

## Noche Oscura

Pain is a hermit's cell stripped bare for you, it is claimed, for your solitary
contemplation, thick walls, windowless, an iron bed, no outside
world for you to hear or see, no beauty to sustain you, where mercy
might arrive to strain all laws of sense, to justify all the good that has died.

It is the silence of the Absolute, the ineffable, unspeakable
extremity of unknowing, the wound of which the mystics write
as a manifestation of God's absence, the corporeal, palpable
denial of meaning, the howl that cries inside you like wolves in the night.

I remember as a boy–this is near nonsense, this trivial, bitter
little allegory–though in a way it tells the truth of the first real hurt
I knew–lucky in most respects as I was growing up–free
of more obvious sorts of suffering then–those would come later–
how I was called by older boys some deadening names, some hateful, dirt-
y names I can't say–that abide as past torments do throbbing in an old man's body.

### Schumann, Fantasie, Op. 17

Call it folly, the seasonal elation, the soulful irruption of fall's fauvist colors
as they catch fire, begin to blaze. Pine, fir, spruce resinous in the heavy air.
The lucidity of dusk's reign gathers, spills over the hills. A forest floor's
needles, moss, and ferns glow iridescent as batlight. A golden mist. What you'd dare
in the dark if you could. Polish the clouds' quicksilver shine. Embrace an empty moon.

Call it madness, love's nocturnal passion. Dismiss it as romanticism. How night
lingers, suspended in the sky. Autumn is the season of dying, they say,
of flying away. Two lovers depart by a bend in the road. It is not right,
it is not just they separate. Yet, look, the trees are unleaving faster each day,
white hairs grow whiter, and the sun nearing the horizon untethers itself from noon.

## Acrophobia

Driving home from Tahoe on a narrow twisting road
overlooking the lake, a drop of a thousand feet
or more from the grassless, crumbling shoulder, you showed
how oblivious you were to my fear we were about to meet
our maker as you combed your white gold hair in the rearview
mirror, your left hand barely gripping the wheel, each curve
taken with the skill of race car driver while I imagined us two
abysmally plummeting though you cooly kept going on pure nerve.

Maybe life is mostly made of a kind of madness. Recklessness.
A dreaming of other's dreams. Summer nights
in Tahoe can be cold as winter. I see
us in our long johns, sleepless
in Marco's rented house, my fear of heights
calmed by your displays of daring, my love for those days, for you and our folly.

## Another Twilight

A late November early evening quiet, breathless as it anticipates sunset.
The woods across the road slope down toward a winding, shallow
creek. Hickory, pine, pin oak, white oak, maple branches form a tight net
against the sky, gnarly vines, tangled ivy, mossy loam, thick ferns below.

He watches from his window, the sun itself invisible behind the thicket
of leafless limbs and spiky needles. On his brand new record player,
he is listening to Eileen Farrell singing Brunhilde's Immolation—unforget-
tably, he thinks. The light filtered through first brightens, then grows dimmer.

Yellow. Orange. A blood red that darkens to scarlet or a somber, fiery maroon.
Darkness fast follows, full night falling just as the music stops. Magically.
He's seventeen. He senses life is a motion picture he can screen, though too soon
over, a film made more moving by the scores he chooses as if it's an old silent movie.

Or a documentary without any family, friends in it about night, the coming of night,
night after night, the beautiful way day has of dying time after time in late fall.
What will his dreams be like when he has grown old far away as the last twilight
of his life begins to fail? What scenes replay so not to fear the splendid terror of it all?

## Learning Reverence

*1.*

Thirteen, camping out with fellow scouts, a wanderer, anxious, sleepless,
the boy waited out the night hidden in a forest until the eastern horizon burned
amber red under an ash gray sky. Its distant fires quickened, seemed to bless
the day as it faded, decayed into mist steaming off the meadow, sun-summoned.

*2.*

Branches, leaves, trunks, massive trees being transformed, tossed, broken
by rain and wind until the thrill of a sky ripped open to the sun
wakes his eyes to a secret he does not know how to keep. Feels bidden
to speak of. How woods grow darker, wilder when storm-wracked by devotion.

*3.*

On sweltering summer nights, he sneaks out his bedroom window, climbs
over a fence to the lake by his home where he ditches his clothes, swims
laps until he tires. Almost sleeps. His naked dripping body is white. Rhymes
with moonlight, pale reeds, or the rimless stuff that spills out it too bright to be sins.

*4.*

Like a prayer, not magic, he repeats his lost friends' names—Luke, Ikey—dead
at sixteen, killed at the wheel of their hot rods by the dog leg turn
they failed to make on a dark country road as if doomed to do it, led
there by the grove or pine stand they careened into where God watches them burn.

*5.*

Late at night, as he walks his dog around the lake, only a last graceful white heron
remains awake, wading its edges, seeking its nest boys destroyed. Mallards, geese
sleep in the reeds. What drove mean kids to kill its young? Starlit waters glisten
darkly. The bird glides through silt like a dancer. Flies off. Is, like him, what it leaves.

## The Day

*1.*
The sun is pale,
flat above
a broken horizon

rising, sail-
ing out of
dark. Its blazon-

ing thick light,
a rain or mist-like
gray, flames yellow.

Dying night-
like shadows strike
incisive strokes below

the hills, trees'
calligraphy
brushed the ancient ways,

as ink frees
a mind to see
its clarity is day's.

*2.*
In the park,
a late September
summer burns the leaves

and grass dark
as amber,
sap or bark, deceives

eyes with
its brightness,
the light flaked like rust.

For the fifth
day, its heat press-
es down on air, too dust-

y to breathe,
the body
oppressed by its bril-

liance, its seething,
sheer white
sky by noon, the shrill-

ness of it,
a sublimity
nearly unbearable,

the way ahead lit
not to see
but be incredible.

3.
The walk back
home damp and muggy,
the doubt that returns,

the void, lack,
loss only,
nothing, what one learns

by looking
reality
too visible maybe,

everything
so simply
what it is, the sea,

the sun blank
white at noon,
its light piercingly hot,

the rot, rank,
of raccoon
or rat, nothing not

sure, the path
underfoot,
the canopy, the birds

or the wrath
to come one fears, the route,
the way, the last words

heard empty,
no new
vision, just forsakenness,

like Jesus' unanswerable plea,
sabachthani,
and so the consoling bless-

ing that silence
can be,
yes, the day's hushed yes.

## Young Oedipus in Corinth

I dream of my father coming at me in the attic of the palace with a knife in his hand.
I dream of a wife whose eyes in a mirror cause it to break into tears like hers.
Tempted by an abyss like the comforts of bed, I slip from sight. I don't understand
what the name I was given augurs, why my foot swells, why my youth is full of fears.

I pick up children in my arms. Hold them tightly, lovingly as I do the mother I embrace.
I am proud of my prick, staff stiff. A blind man lurks in my sleep, his beard spittle gray.
I lie to him. I say I never trip when I am constantly falling. Lose like a girl every race.
The old women in the plaza weep. Speak the name of some strange city. Sing. Pray.

In the morning, words spill from my mouth like a great king's on their own.
As I bathe, my nakedness shines like the sun become human.
My father praises my promise, my bravery, my precocious eloquence.

But a boy, he advises, is like a seed in a well-tended garden the gods have sown.
Or seedling olive trees they have planted. Pain is destined, part of their plan.
Rage against it reverently. An unknown fate awaits you. Be led to its grove by silence.

## A Last Heron on Hamilton Lake in Late November

It is not the end of autumn that prevents me in my old age from sleeping
but the smell of smoke from burning leaves in my father's backyard.
Night after night the sound of rain. Night after night cold winds blowing.
It is not reality that keeps me from dreaming, the truths that make life hard.

How lonely is the evening as it settles on the bridge over the creek near the lake.
The days rush as swiftly by, and my prayers stay unanswered. Heresy
is the pond where a blue heron fishes by a pine stand. I write for the sake
of my dead father. To tell him I remain a believer. A heron wading alone and winter-
  ready.

PETER WELTNER was raised in northern New Jersey and piedmont North Carolina. He graduated from Hamilton College (A.B.) and Indiana University (Ph.D.) and taught British, Irish, and American literature at San Francisco State for thirty-seven years. He has published twenty books or chapbooks of fiction or poetry. His work has appeared in several national anthologies, including two O. Henry's. He lives with his husband, Atticus Carr, steps away from the Pacific in San Francisco.

www.ingramcontent.com/pod-product-compliance
Lightning Source LLC
Chambersburg PA
CBHW021956290426
44108CB00012B/1094